I RISE TO YOUR LIGHT

PRAISE FOR THE POETRY AND ART OF
SARAH SUZANNE NOBLE

"Sarah's work is exquisite. The combination of breathtaking photography and eloquent poetry make this a joyful read. I can't recommend it enough."

Steve Hoppe
pastor, counselor, author of *Sipping Saltwater* and *Marriage Conflict: Talking as Teammates*

"Sarah is a beautiful example of bringing the pains and cares of life to God in lament as well as praise, finding beauty in everyday life, listening and responding with creativity, honesty, and hope."

Catherine Lawton
poet, author of *Glimpsing Glory* and *Remembering Softly*

"[Sarah's poetry] is fully incarnated in concrete imagery. I like the transparency of feeling. The words and lines flow beautifully. The photographs are stunning."

Leland Ryken
author, professor of English at Wheaton College

"In this age filled with desperation and deception, it is a joy to see and experience the truthful, simple beauty of God's love and care for us. His tender mercies are poignantly and thoughtfully presented with the smallest of details. Thank you for this mindful reflection of God's blessings."

Paul Konrad
WGN Television Personality and speaker

"Sarah gives voice to the rawness and reality of life that so many of us feel yet are not able to express."

Jackson Crum
pastor

"In our own seasons of suffering, words to explain the pain, to cry out to God, or to get a grip on our faith are often hard to come by. We tend to throw our brains into neutral—not wanting to admit our inadequacies before God or anyone else. In our dark days, Sarah's paintings, photography, and hopeful words of comfort add color and life to our souls and give words to our own reality. Above all else is the peace found when we acknowledge that 'He's been there all along—and we dwell secure.'"

Elaine Wright Colvin
WIN

"This collection of Scripture-inspired poems and photographs gives a window into Sarah Noble's creative and captivating mind while moving the reader to worship. Whether by verse or by image, Sarah's artwork stirs the soul."

John Goodrich
author, assistant professor at Moody Bible Institute

"Wonderful book of poetry, enhanced by Sarah's paintings and photographs. As a pastoral counselor, I can't wait to commend her book to the many people who are suffering and struggling to give words to their physical and emotional pain. I wish I had access to her books at the times in my life when I was struggling with my own emotional pain. The poetry is raw and real and yet infused with hope, beauty and faith."

Dr. Bill Meier
Pastoral Counselor and Professor.

"[Sarah's poems] reflect the lament, transparency and hope of the Psalms."

Donna Crum
Global Team, Park Community Church

I RISE TO YOUR LIGHT

Poetic Meditations

Sarah Suzanne Noble

CLADACH
Publishing

I RISE TO YOUR LIGHT
Poetic Meditations
©2022 by Sarah Suzanne Noble

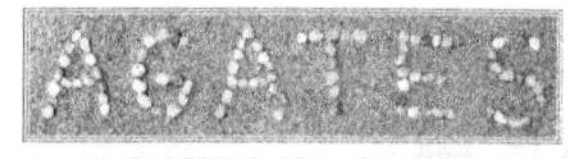

An AGATES Book of Poetry

Published by Cladach Publishing
Greeley, Colorado 80633
https://cladach.com
All rights reserved.

Cover Photo and Interior Photos: Sarah Suzanne Noble
Author Photo: Rob Clements

"In the Grey" (p. 17) was first published and anthologized in
The Animals In Our Lives: Stories of Companionship and Awe
(Cladach, 2021).

ISBN: 978-1-945099-32-8
Library of Congress Control Number: 2022948951

Printed in the United States of America

TABLE OF CONTENTS

INTRODUCTION

*He who runs from God in the morning will scarcely
find Him the rest of the day.*

–John Bunyan

I have written much in this past season of Covid, but this work adjoins my previous work *I Cry Unto You O Lord* from winter 2019 to winter 2020, the years leading up to the pandemic.

As I reviewed this work to confirm its relevancy, I was struck by how prayers of lament and praise weave through time regardless of world events. Every morning we rise, and every morning we are reminded that our Father's compassions and mercies are new each day. Because of His great love we are not consumed. Because of His faithfulness we are not alone in this world. He is our Sustainer, whether it's 2019 or 2022.

We as believers journey together through this life, eagerly awaiting the next. Where our aches, pains, and suffering shall cease and we will rest in His glorious presence. With this hope and with this lens I write.

To paint the year leading to the pandemic and the prayers and songs written in this book, I will give a quick review of my health history and my family.

Spring of 2019, I was a thirty-five year old mother of two: Ruthie, age five, and Jacob, age three. We were living in a condo in Ukrainian Village Chicago, Illinois. Work had brought my husband and me to this city in 2008. God had made clear in 2013 that he had and still has work for us to do in this place. Yielding my vision of life in the countryside, we settled in and began the great work of raising children. By this point a myriad of illnesses had bubbled up and become chronic ailments. My typical days were and are filled with two weeks of migraines per month, back and neck structural issues, and the remnants of PPD with its anxiety and insomnia.

The environment was and is challenging for raising children. Neighbors below, beside, in back. Stairs, always stairs, to reach anywhere in Chicago. And small spaces, which often meant packing children up to release energy at nearby parks. So this is the season in which I wrote this work, *I Rise to Your Light*. In between recovering, in between nights, in between toddler fights. But God was faithful in this season. The Lord provided creative opportunities that made my heart hum. He used Jonny and me to teach and mentor lots of young men and women. He allowed us to grow, to plant, to create, and for part of 2019, to rest.

What was to follow this season of recovery, was 2020. Which meant homeschooling toddlers, playing in alleys and parking lots due to park closures, zoom prayer calls, unattended funerals, and an emergency back fusion in October.

Life is a series of peaks, valleys, and plains. In my writing I attempt to give language to these times of joy, sorrow, and waiting; with the hope to call us higher each morning, to look up and wonder, to behold something beautiful, to thank God for who he is, for what he has done and who he will forever be.

I often read Oswald Chambers' *My Utmost for His Highest*. A portion of that book's reading for July 20 is a fitting conclusion here:

*Having the reality of God's presence is not dependent
on our being in a particular circumstance or place,
but is only dependent on our determination to keep
the Lord before us continually.*

May each of us keep the Lord before us continually,
and by His grace we will rise to His light each morning.

Fondly,

Sarah Suzanne Noble

I.
RISE

In the Grey

In the grey
I see a red bird
A cardinal
Roosting on chair

He stares
Right in my eye
As I stretch
As my muscles ache

He stares
The rain drops fall
In April
A snowstorm a day ago

He stares
Buds limp from cold
Petals on floor
God, you stare.

You see me in the waiting
Thank you for the bird
That stares.
A reminder that you

Are everywhere.
And at the same time
With me in grey
Hope for the day.

Hints of Hope

Daily we are called
Daily we are sent
To be hints of hope.
To reflect our maker
As the dew drops
Mirror the green grass
As a child repeats
Prayers from the past.
Lord Jesus give us
Our daily bread,
Forgive us from
The evils said,
The thoughts of
Thanklessness and fear.
Help us be hints of hope
In this world you love so dear.

Clouds

Clouds are the dust of his feet.

If clouds are but dust
How big is he?
Veiled is He
Radiant Glory
Mighty strong hands
Grasping mountains,
Craftsman precision,
Forming Adam
Surgically Steady
A Rib for Eve.

Clouds are the dust of his feet.

Almighty is He
Beyond compare,
Above our air
Infinite reign
Mars is but a
Marble in hand.
Voice thunders trees
Collapsing knees
Wind he breathes
Stars placed high.

Clouds are the dust of his feet.

Spring Forth

Spring forth my soul into shouting!
Legs leap into gleeful galloping.
Hands clap with the rhythm of trees.
Body collapse onto my knees.
Tears pour like the summer rain.
Mind recalls my victors claim.
Death is defeated,
Christ is enough.
To conquer sin, and rise us up.
We dance with our Lord at His Feast.
A wedding banquet rose with yeast.
Passover complete, praise we repeat.
Spring forth my soul into shouting!

Glorify You

Father, how I can glorify you?
Help me praise you as I wait.
Bring to mind Christ's cost.
Bring to mind saints scoffed.

Rejoice oh my soul
Rejoice in the cold
Rejoice in the sunset
Rejoice in the not yet

Focus on the Father
Focus on His Word
Focus on the Truth

Sing of the past
Sing in the present

Guard hearts from resentment
Guard thoughts from serpent lies

Help your servant to be wise.
Yield my goals and yield my life
To the Author of all
May he be glorified.

Early Morning

I stretch outside
I feel the breeze
I stare at my toes
I gaze at the trees.

Swaying, beckoning
That I would look up
Not be caught in
Repetitive thought.

I look up and see
The clear blue sky
A comforting color
The blue of an eye.

As I survey the limbs
I watch them move
Shadows dance smooth
Lobes caressed with gold
That shimmers from the sun's glow.

Further down full branch beams
Vibrant moss textured seams
Oh the light it reaches deep
It touches every part of the tree.
Soon it will rest on me.

Blessings Counted

One tree in my yard
Two children in my car
Three rooms with beds
Four tummies fed
Five years on this street
Six marriage retreats
Seven chairs for friends
Eight vertebrae now bend
Nine neighbors' smiles
Ten toes walk miles
Eleven pots on deck
Twelve herb scents
Thirteen paintings lay
Fourteen collage displays
Fifteen paper hearts
Sixteen doodles of art
Seventeen hugs per day
Eighteen times I pray
Nineteen songs we sing
The counted blessings are unending.

Crab Apple Tree

Crab apple trees
Sway in the breeze
Petals late
but present
Spring flutters
Lost laments
Envelope pink
Life abounds
Winter white
Now color
Song birds chirp
Barren branch
Another chance
Preordained
Marching dance
Flowers fall
Apples born
Fruit produced
Suns warmth
Juicy tart
Red hearts
Reminder
Remember
Mercies taste
In late fall November

Seeds of Faith

Seeds sprout in dirt
They unfold in weeks.
Covered in germs
Then release.

Rise up inch by inch
Seed is now a hat.
The sprout gets tall
Than lies flat.

It must be pinched
To spread the growth
For roots to go
Sideways in the soil.

The plant endures
It's footing sure.
Outside it goes
To test true light
To harden a bit
But taken in at night.

Quickly it adjusts
To the whirls of dust
It flourishes now
In its wide pot
Soaking up the rays
Enjoying the hot.

Our seeds of faith
Indeed are similar
They require protection
They need to be nursed
They need to be tried
In order to flourish

I Arise Today

I arise today
To the scent of flower sweet
To cool breeze at my feet.

I arise today
To the morning star nigh
To a gradient of light.

I arise today
To mercies pure and fresh
To new life, defeat of death.

I arise today
Reborn because of grace
Revitalized, may I taste.

I arise today
By your body and blood
By broken bread, wine in cup.

I arise today
Waters wash me through
Spirit rests in me anew.

I arise today
To bow before my King
To serve you and to sing

II.
REFLECTION

What is mankind that you are mindful of them,
human beings that you care for them?

Psalm 8:4

My Life Is a Song

My life is a Song
Notes may tarry
Low it seems
But soon rise
With he who redeems
Notes may stall
Mid stanza awhile
But triumphantly build
To the Holy Child
Verse by verse
A song is written
Of a people lost
A people forgiven
The refrain repeats
Graces anew
The music unfolds
To a song prelude
My life is a song
With its ups and downs
Written long ago
To my Father's tune
Beautiful it is
Composed with care
A melody of worship
Lingers in the air

Sweat on Brow

We work by the sweat
of our brow, and stench.

We sow the seeds
and watch them grow
through the thorns,
the weeds and thistle.
We harvest the food
our God provides;
We work together
at each other's side.

Vocation, a calling
to be the Lord's people,
to work the sod,
to hum the feeble
melodies of work
and rhythms of rest;
directed by our Father
Who knows us best.

Birds of Air

Birds of air
Lay their nest
Cover their eggs
With feathered breast

Store not they
Worms in the wood
Seeds in the branches
Packets of food

Yet the Father cares
He provides
He knows what's inside
Of the delicate egg

A baby who needs fed
A mother who needs strength
A father who searches at length
A God who provides
For the robin, the jay
The butterfly

Consider the Lilies

Consider the lilies
Stars like stalks
Rising to greet the morn
Bursting colors
Seeded Scarlet, golden ray
Mauve's pinkness
White's meekness
They toil not
They spin not
Yet brilliant
More royal than robed men
David's Son
Even grander than Solomon
Scent of sweet
Wafted breeze
Arrayed sight
Without worry
Lightly flutter
Humbly bow
Oh Consider
The lilies
Of the field
Right now

Juniper

Juniper
Star of hope
Blue needles
Absorb the
Harsh sun rays
Shade display

Found in dry
Desert spaces
Shepherds drink
Sheep will rest
Hunger pains
Roots eaten

Juniper
Star of hope
Shelter provided
Our
Hopes
Confided

Hyssop

Wash me Lord
Forgive my sin
Branch of hyssop
Enter in

Mint cleansing
Brush spreading
Wipe the blood
Across the door

Passover Lamb
Preparation plan
Branch so long
It offers gull

Tinged with wine
To our Savior
The Humble Lamb
The Great I Am.

Old Testament
To the New
Trains us for
Enduring truth

A cleansing branch
Another chance
Hyssop grows
It's frame cleans

Angel Armies

Angel Armies
Legions of Fire

Messengers of God
Obedience required

Servants of the Lord
 Sweet songs they breathe

More brilliant than stars
Such powerful beings

Created by God
For worshipping

An Army in
Hand of Trinity

Power can't compare
With root of Jesse

Bedroom

Bedroom as sanctuary
In bedroom I pray
Bedroom as hospital
In bedroom I lay
Bedroom as workshop
In bedroom I create
Bedroom as meeting place
A bedroom of grace
Bedroom as covenant
Our bedroom of love
Bedroom, you've been
Restored from above

God in the Valley

The most likely course is the Valley.
The low point, the flatlands, the abbey.
We seek you, Lord, with our back at the wall.

When there is darkness in shame we crawl.
The Valley is shadowed by mountains tall.
The sun hidden for days I recall.

You call us forward, beyond frightening stuff.
To a ridge where we can see,
Our God three in One, Holy Trinity.

As we journey on, help us not forget,
This Valley pilgrimage is temporary,
As we yearn for the not yet.

More than Me

Today is about more than me
I confess my sorrow and jealousy

Father thank you that the earth spins
It's marked course around the sun
That mercies arrive with the dawn

Father thank you that you are my core.
You are my worth you humble me.
The earth requires the sun to see.

Vision for the future, wisdom from the past.
Directing my course, a revolving path.

Of you at the center, repentance on my knees.
Sins forgiven, now I am living sight on eternity.

Deep Breath

Deep Breath, air enters in
Exhale decay and sin.
Repetitious, relentless
The pulsating breath
Produced by an organ of red.
Lungs expand, open hands.
Muscles relinquish control.
Mind wanders to the fruit that was stole.
Apple in hand or perhaps persimmons.
Permission not granted when roots
Have plans, seeking direction in sand.
Storms churn and turn,
lost in a desert, lies from a worm.

Fruit of control becomes applesauce,
sweet to taste but then squashed.
Seeds lost no more bearing,
enter fear, resentment and comparing.
Father breathe your life in my dirt,
your moisture in my dust.
Resurrect this body, this chest.
Help me breathe deep, see you holy, complete.
Creator, Sustainer. Preserver, Savior.

Prayer

Father, take me to that Holy Place,
Where olive branches encircle your face.
Where fervent prayer see,
the perspective of eternity.
Where moments are but a page,
Of the unending story of grace.
I need your help in the seeking,
In the humbling, in the creeping.
Dust I taste, mixed with salt smears.
Tears held by a hardened heart,
separating the sorrowful parts.
Cancer, tumors, disease.
Loved ones on bended knees.
Weeping below willow trees.
Sunsets of red bleed at night.
Whispers of cold seeping cries.
Weights press down holding a frown.
Brightness breaks the doldrums.
Sunshine shatters the sorrows.
Spirit soars to great heights.
Jesus helps me in this fight!
Father bestows boldness in prayer.
Soul rejoices in Christ my Savior.
Help me see your Holy face,
Encircled with olive branches,
A sign of grace.

Geode

Lord, I cannot see what's hidden.
Crack my shell formed by pressure.
I feel chips and aging,
Like a tombstone for engraving.

Chilly skin, cracking hands,
Winter not over yet.
Vomit stains, sweat soaked sheets;
Will a baby bird chirp in me?

Is there beauty beyond measure,
Ultimate treasure inside of me?
When the weight rolls me to the ground,
Will my husk flake?

Carapace removed, armor breaking,
Reveal in me your Holy Spirit.
Glittering core, fortified rock,
Crystals galore, shimmer shock.

Vision on Cross

Lord, you gave me a vision from the cross.
I saw John consoling my mother for her loss.
The men beside me smelt of death.
Trying to push up on the nails for breath.
The soldiers spit felt cool.
It dripped with my bloody stool.
Venomous words formed around me.
In the choking the air I could hardly breathe.
The mourning of Mary, Lazarus, and Martha.
The morning star sinking downward.
Disciples wailing, the sky dressed in black.
Awaiting the funeral of the First and the Last.
The Lamb of God, slaughtered flesh.
"It is finished," I yell with what's left in my chest.
My eyes roll back, the ultimate death.
Immediately I descend to Sheol.
To the servants tunnel or horror.
The moaning, the scratching and screams.
Nightmare of nightmares, but not a dream.
The weight of sin crushes, it bruises my heels.
The power of the Trinity I now feel.
Return of the Father, unyielding power.
The serpent retreats; he squirms in defeat.
Victor over vanquished, Omnipotent has overcome.
Prophecy fulfilled, Savior raised in Glory.
Disciples believe the unending story.

Why

So often I ask why:
Why the rain, why this time
Why now, looking behind
The whys lead nowhere
They loop round and round
Spin like a top, dig in the ground
Perspective is off
Why forgets its place, a bit like a scoff
Instead of praise, it questions authority
Presuming supremacy, balking at God

I must kneel, let my crust peel
Expose my flesh, receive sweet rest
Repent of control, release concern
Be a student once more, able to learn
Accept the path, the trail, the plan
The voyage slated, direction to man

Praise you that you know all
That you see small and tall
That you have a vision for me
Obedience brings joy
Finally free

What's Next

What's next? Mind churns
Forgetting lessons learned
Reaching towards illusions
Left with confusion

Grasping green grapes
Not yet sweet to taste
Running on rocks
Lost in the flock

Forgetting my place
My tail I chase
Direct me straight
Help me wait

For future fulfillments
Recall past merriments
Victory already won
Not by me; by the Son

So I may live with peace
Radiate joy
Serve others
Sinner savoy

Good Gifts

Thank you for home
Thank you for children
For clear provision

Thank you for spouse
Thank you for marriage
For all that I cherish

Thank you for work
Thank you for schools
For art supply tools

Thank you for friends
Thank you for family
For tree canopy

Thank you for health
Thank you for sweet foods
For pains removed

Thank you for gifts
Thank you for seeing
For redeeming

Aspire

Aspirations for God's glory
Good gifts used to tell the story
Continue on, persevere
Produce fruitfulness this year
Watch it grow, watch it tread
As years pass, as you lay your head
Keep in mind the gifts are good
And the Lord produces the food
Aspire each day, seek His face
Remember to lean on His grace.

Discourage

Discouraged in waiting, clouds heavy
Work in vain, it seems gray surrounds
Delight is hidden, frowns are heavy
First drops fall, then a downpour

I cry out to you, Lord, author of the sky
I seek your celestial face; it shines bright
Stuck here in mire, I bow to your light
You reach into the muck, gently lift me up

Lend courage to the lowly, breathe life slowly
Revive the hardened, soothe the swollen
Wind's whispers mend, its shout bends
Heart back on track, now help me to sing

Patience

Completely humble
Gentleness
Slow to speak
Faithfulness
Perseverance
Perspective
Disciplined
Reflective
Light on a hill
Oil in lamp
Bridegroom arrival
Peaceful patience

When Needs Are Great

When needs are great, I lower my head
The weight of the task, the journey ahead
Fear of slipping, fear of equipping

Saints and sinners, to deliver dinners
Gravity strong, my face is long
Lord lift me up, help me see your cup

A life of service, a life of care
A life that's worthy, a life of prayer

A Father who's present, the spirit evident
The cross created, the task of being hated
The procession forward

Glory that's restored, strength to walk
Wisdom to pray, hope moving forward
Into a new day

Megaphone

Rise up my soul
Hear the melody
The song my Savior sings for me

Rise up my soul
Through the pain
Megaphone of grace calls my name

Ears often closed
Mind tends to wander
In self-absorbed pity, time squandered

Rise up my soul
Hear the birds call
Repetition repents, I kneel to you now

Rise up my soul
Remember the tune
Underserved love on the cross for you

The Christian Walk

The Christian walk knows suffering
    It draws near to the broken
    It picks up the piercing
    And by God's grace amends

The Christian walk can fill with tears
    For friends lost, family seeking
    For boggy days, deep sludge
    For patient waiting

The Christian walk fills with joy
    Of love true and tried, fellowship side by side
    Of encouragement, of pointing
    Of oil poured out for anointing

The Christian walk leads to Christ
    To all other things falling at his side
    To visions of future rest, to prayers
    To a high priest who hears request

III.
DELIGHT

He brought me out into a spacious place; he rescued me because he delighted in me.

Psalm 18:19

Joy Beyond Measure

Joy beyond measure
Infinite pleasure
In your presence, Lord
You fill my form

Lips laced with praise
Eyes that can see
Author Illustrator
Of the yet to be

Composer of crickets
Melodious rib-its
In unison
Worshipping

A spring that overflows
Jubilant mist
Cooling the grass
A Sweet respite

Thoughts of my King
His splendor and crown
Make my soul leap
My joy abound

Pulse

The ocean has a pulse
A rhythmic beat
Praising effortlessly
Heart of the ocean
Stored in ground
Hear the waves chant
A soothing sound
A pulse of praise
Lest we forget
Our creator, restorer
Beyond a net
Higher than the stars
Deeper than divides
Thunder as voice
The wind he rides
All creation has a pulse
Lest we forget

Friendship

Across race, across miles
Bound by trials
Smiles of understanding
Open Hands of giving

Fellow workers unite
A faithful God they recite
Worship song and psalm
Makes the body strong

Laughter in candor, reminders too
Of a shared vision united by truth
Journey on, faithful friend
Run your race, don't bend

Straight towards our Savior's Hand
Reach for it in all your plans
Remember the God of Goodness
Who called you from nothingness

To raise you up, to fill your cup
To place you with saints
Who run the same race, with
Encouragement to our final home.

Friendship built on Earth
Forever in paradise to worship.

Witness

My eyes witness miracles
My heart feels mending

Marriages restored
Marriages remembering

Christ who reconciles
Grace upon grace

When challenges overwhelm
And we lose our sense of pace

Travel on the path
Step by step

Lamp lights the way
Lest we forget

Hand in hand
Couples renewed

The improbable
Becomes new

Brilliant faces testify
To The Worker of Wonder

Sisters in Christ

A true Blessing
Sisters in Christ
Meeting in morning
Encouraging at night
Present in the pain
Sorrow and delights
Cool drops of rain
In the midst of the fight
Lips laced with wisdom
Not self-propelled might
A crown of friends
Encircles my head
Helmets of truth
That speaks in my stead
Tongues gently teach
Arms that embrace
In the joy and grief
Lights that glow
On an advent wreath

At Rest

I talk to you Lord
At rest
I drink your word
At rest
I hear you call
At rest
I feel so small
At rest
You rain on me
At rest
You pour out freely
At rest
You breathe life in me
At rest
You dwell divine
Eternally

Love that Compels

Love that Compels
    relentlessly
Love that Claims
    my entirety
Love that Forgives
    my iniquity
Love that Sets
    me free
Love that Sustains
    my heart
Love that Seeks
    and finds
Love that Embraces
    faithfully
Love that Securely
    graces
My life
    and yours

Sweet Grace

Sweet Grace
  May it resound
Sweet Grace
  It's the only sound
Sweet Grace
  It draws me near
Sweet Grace
  Remove my fears
Sweet Grace
  From God above
Sweet Grace
  Undeserved love
Sweet Grace
  Is all I see
Sweet Grace
  Christ in me

One Thousand

One thousand leaves
Clap in the sky
One thousand petals
Absorb light
One thousand birds
Chirp a song
One thousand rocks
Carefully formed
One thousand spots
On just one cat
One thousand smiles
On those that laugh
One thousand words
One stupendous Savior
One thousand stars
One endless deliverer

Greet

Hello, we smile.
Neighbors we greet.

Fresh air,
Relinquish care.

Strangers meet,
because of beauty.

Common graces,
intersect new faces.

We hope to meet again.
Until then

The Lords favor
Rest on you, my friend.

Eyes Full of Tears

Eyes full of tears, beauty I cannot taste
Surrounded by green in this urban place

The hum of a car rests in the back
Through misty eyes I gaze plant racks

Sedums brilliant green, blue and red
Terra cotta pots nestled next to me

Cactus spikes, Barberry's red
Lilacs purple, beautiful rest

In the distance I hear melody
Ice cream truck in city streets

Thank you, Lord, that we still meet
When path is hard, surface concrete

Thank you familiar scents abound
Senses delight as I look around

Eyes full of tears, I recall you are here—
Meeting needs freshly, sweetly, intimately

Bird Song

Bird song
Curved plants
Red leaves
Incense
Patterned dots
Rippled pots
Moss cracks
Woven seat
Temperate
Gentle breeze
Silent respite
Relief, wonder, delight
My soul speaks

Lily of the Valley

It took so long to meet
Your bells of white
Your flowers petite.
A scent so sweet
It draws wide smile.
Smile in a Valley?
Lily, you make no sense!
How could there be
Treasure in lowliness?
Where sun shifts
Where shadows linger
Where canyons tall
Claw at my fingers.
There you dwell
In the shade,
in the muck;
Beacons of light
Dots like lady bugs.
Lord, thank you for lilies,
Delicates in the valley.

IV.
SETBACK

*Not only so, but we also glory in our sufferings,
because we know that suffering produces perseverance;
perseverance, character; and character, hope. And hope
does not put us to shame, because God's love has been
poured out into our hearts through the Holy Spirit,
who has been given to us.*

Romans 5: 3-5

Slide

Vertebrae slide out of place,
Pain creeps on my face.
Patience slides out of place,
Anger towards little faces.

Forgive me, Lord, for my lack,
For gentleness cracking,
For harsh words and looks,
For despising my work.

Knead this stiffness
Into warm clay.
Help me bend to your ways,
To stop, to listen,

To pray for forgiveness
To reconcile, seek,
To exchange brash for meek,
To remain, not slide.

Construction paper card,
Pink folded in half
Her letters inside,
Hearts layered in grass.

Starry sky mass,
A flower for mother.
We both repent,
Steadfast Father.

Mirrors

Mirrors crash down
Shatter on the floor
Surround my weak mortal form

Lord, break the lies
The false rejections
Help me see beyond my imperfections

Shards of glass
Fall oh, so slowly
Tempered lies retain a form

I tried to stand
Against my Lord
Jesus Christ sets me free

Free am I
Oh, free indeed!
No more bondage to fear

No mirrors now
Only a tear
Drops of grace roll down my face

Amazing Grace
Now I can see
Demolished myth, exposed falsity.

Stuck

Feet in mud
I feel stuck

Caught to my knees, I sink further
Deep, Deep muck

Plans flawed, skin raw
Though it tarries, wait

Look up to the sky
"Yield," He says. Delay is respite

Hiatus is recess, stoppage is break
Idle is abiding, stuck is remaining

Feet in the mud
I let them soak

Evil Surrounds

When evil surrounds, I look towards You
When the enemy is in pursuit

When it looks like waywardness wins
When it seems there is only sin

When evil surrounds, I look towards you
Author, Perfector of all truth

Healer, Priest-King of eternity
There is nothing Your eyes can't see

In the mess You work to restore
Our city, our land. You are Lord

Lord, Lift Me

Lord, lift me up
Above towers and dust
To skies of powder blue,
To beauty and truth
Lord, lift me towards your face
To be empowered by grace

Child, It Will Be All Right

"Child, it will be all right.
Aches are but moments in the journey of life.
Joys are numerous, beauty abounds.
Eyes untrained look down."

I see dirt, I see trash,
I see my failures, I itch a rash.

"Child look up," *speaks in my ear.*
Father wipes away the tears.

"Look, I have made wheat dance,
The crow that calls, deer who prance.
Child, it will be all right,
Rest in my warmth and might.
Count the stars if you can,
Sift your fingers through sand,
Witness lightning, hear thunder.
Are you beginning to wonder?
Broaden your sight, child, see my might.
Gasp in awe at what I've made."

Help Me See Glory

Help me see glory
In this dark place
My feet stumble
May I behold your face

Help me see glory
In the everyday
Light of Ages
A continual display

Remind me of radiance
Remind me of brilliance
Remind me of conquest
Remind me of holiness

Help me see glory
In your word, in my life
Help me rejoice
At a Savior glorified

Ache

Blankets wrap
Around me
Ache breaks
My rope
Downward I sink
Covered in sores
The salty waves sting
Ocean of life
Encapsulates me
Without my anchor
I am drowning
Caught in pity
Tossed by anger
Looking down
Tempest danger
Beacon of Hope
rescue my flesh
May my body heal
And be refreshed.
Light in soul
Forever glow
Garments of white
Preserve life
Eternal covering

Winter Lingers

The cold lingers
My sprouts shrink
The clouds cover
My spirit sinks
The child sick
So much Suffering
House as haven
House as Petri dish
Under attack
The enemy's wish
Germs I cannot see
I know they exist
Satan prowls the same
With risen fists
Unseen but present
Underestimated tyrant
Coy he is, hidden he seems
Whispering lies and fallacy
Baiting me to doubt
That the Father's good
Pecking at my patience
Woodpecker to the wood
He wants me to slip
Grumble and quit
This season will end
Soon the sun will shine
And seeds may be sown

Alone

When I lie on cool sheets
I pray for peace and relief

I yearn to see you at my side
Christ my Savior, do not hide

I want you and nothing more
To nestle in your wings secure

To look out from your towers
To worship for hours

As sheep sleep, you guard the pen.
Protecting my life, forgiving my sin.

When I feel alone, help me recall.
You are my ever-present all in all.

Dry Bones

Lord, breathe into my bones
They lie dry and without hope
Spread in the Valley
Dust has no home

Searching, swirling for life
No branch to cling to
No spot to rest, only blowing
Seedless sowing, unglued

Lord breathe into my bones
The breathe of the living
From the four winds
May I rejoice with thanksgiving

Tendons form muscles
Skin envelopes this form
Crafted by my Maker
Carried by my mother

Even storms bring rain
Help me, Lord; I feel slain
Lord breathe into my bones
Feed with your bread

Yearn

I yearn for this headache to fade
For sunshine instead of gray

I seek hope, I seek joy
Daffodils one inch tall

When will they flower?
I watch them every hour

Nausea gone, taste buds savor
Flavors of coffee and butter

Strong flavor or salty taste
My desire as my body wastes

Am I looking to the wrong place?
At the blessings and not the grace?

Lift me higher so I can see,
All that Christ has done for me.

Light the dark, and pierce the fog,
Help me to have vision.

Help me to hear the chime
And thank you for this sweet time.

Shake

In the waiting, I shake
Thoughts quake
Fears erupt
I am stuck

In a cycle of spinning
Am I winning?
Faster the pace
Veritable race

In the waiting, I seek
My Heart pleads:
Guard mind relapse
Journeys from past.

Draw from past triumphs
Remember promises.
Faithful is my keeper,
Faithful is my leader.

Weary

Swollen knee
Soft sheets
Twitching thigh
Blue sky

Tight headache
Pillow shade
Blinded bliss
Boned entrance

Take heart hope
The enemy prowls
Taunts provokes
My life is spared

Spacious place
Merciful Savior
My God of Grace,
Set my pace.

Pride

Pride is like a ribbon
Wrapped round a post
Till it unravels
Then we boast
Trying to keep it high
Elevated and pristine
Bow tied neatly
Satin shimmering

So focused on the ribbon
We stare at it for days
Glancing nowhere else
Seeking others' praise
Bragging, swaggering
Screeching saint

Not fit for the title
A sin-tainted trait
Repent Repent
You draw near
I look at My Maker
With a Holy fear

Remove the pride inside
Unwrap the perfect bow
Show me my faults
Let me lie low
Lift me in time
Beyond the little post.
To see your world wide
Father, Son, Holy Ghost

V.
SAVIOR

She will bear a Son; and you shall call His name Jesus,
for He will save His people from their sins.

Matthew 1:21

Pass Through

A decision brews,
A crucial choice
To pass through
The Doorway to life
Covered in blood
Unleavened bread
Bitter herb buds
Readiness not rest
Only darkness
To pass through
Finish the lamb
Eat all you can
Wait for destroyer
To save God's chosen
To journey forward

To pass through
Seas of death
For faith to resurrect
For years to obey
To cast out dismay
To look toward the promised
To enjoy God's Fellowship
To pass through
To Canaan land
To remember God's bread
In the midst of sand
Now at the threshold
What do you choose?

Twilight

Twilight
  Passover Lamb
Twilight
  The Great I Am
Twilight
  Death at dusk
Twilight
  A sacrifice
Twilight
  Spotless Lamb
Twilight
  A gift for man
Twilight
  Darkness three days
Twilight
  My sin he forgave
Twilight
  Pierced in side
Twilight
  Disciples hide
Twilight
  Waiting, then sight

Peril

Dry bones
In desert perils
Dry bones
Satan's peddles
Dry bones
Breath of Life
Dry bones
Christ's sacrifice

Dry bones
Made from dust
Dry bones
Not broken or crushed
Dry bones
Spear in side
Dry bones
Death, then Life

Little Child

Little Child, Father of nations
Little Child, Mother's favorite
Little Child, wrestles God
Little Child, Tribe of Judah
Little Child, born in manger
Little Child, always a stranger
Little Child, a voice calls
Little Child, obedient to death
Little Child, sacrifice of blood
Little Child, redeems the lost
Little Child, releases breath
Little Child, Lion of Light
    Frightful sight, blazing bright
    Defeats night, requires delight
    Full of might, deep and high
    Draw me nigh to abide in
Little Child

Beauty Remains

Beauty remains
Star filled sky
Charcoal nigh
Beauty remains
Laced flurries
Squirrel scurries
Beauty remains
Dandelion dots
Tulip tea cups
Beauty remains
Pale blue storm
Green grass forms
Beauty remains
Waves' heartbeat
Sand, shore, sea
Beauty remains
Given by lowly
Compass toward holy
Beauty remains
Breathed out
So we can breathe in

Whirlwind

I wonder what it would be like lifted up
In a whirlwind, breathe of God;
Creation eddies, Breeze on skin
Lifted by wind. Lungs sing, clothes cling.
Closer, higher I am carried by the sky
To my creator, toward sunshine of His face,
glories of His Son. I wipe away a tear.
Rain falls, then clears. Warmth on face,
No more disgrace. Worship in the whirlwind.
I wonder, oh I wonder. Elijah knows.
Someday I will ask, I suppose.

Sun High Above

Sun high above
It marks midday
I stop and pray

Sun high above
Formed by word
Blazing burst

Sun high above
Guides the day
Creates moon rays

Sun high above
Warms my skin
Gives rest within

Sun high above
Creator higher yet
Lord not beget

Sun high above
Reminder gleams
Follow the sunbeam

I Lay My Head

I lay my head
To pillow soft
To nod off

I lay my head
Prayers said
Needs met

I lay my head
To angel song
Sleep deep, long

I lay my head
Though boat rocks
In storm onslaught

I lay my head
You bestow peace
Remove grief

I lay my head
Great shepherd
Of sheep

I lay my head
Gently guide
Wayward me

Tender Shoot, Dry Root

No majesty or beauty
Despised face
Crushed
In our place
Man of sorrow
Afflicted
Oppressed
Stricken
With the wicked
Guilt offering
For his offspring
After suffering
Light of Life
Knowledge
Righteousness
Spoils for lost
Great sacrifice

On a dry cross

Light

A string of lights
Glows bright
Shines at darkest night

Attacked by swarms
Threatens harm
A buzzing storm

Then dawn breaks
Rays penetrate
Insects fade

Battle then rest
Christ in chest
I shine my best

He fights for me
He holds my ground
When fears resound

He strikes terror
In the enemies' eyes
They must hide

Beam of light
Jewel inside
Saturate sky

Majestic

Majestic, I ponder
Majestic, I wonder
Dignity, Grace
Marvelous Place
Awestruck eyes
Eternal sunrise
Perpetual spring
Mountains bend over
Rivers rise high
Stars glitter down
Coruscating sky
Grasses sway, deer play
Lightning illuminates
Thunder radiates
Rocks cry out and shout
Harmonies heard, sung
By all creation and tongues
Majestic Lord
Reigns Above
Splendor grand
Unfailing Love

Death

Death's drumbeat
Bids us retire
To quit ahead
Repeats the liar

Serpent slithers
Taunts retreat
Stop hoping
Follow me

The tempo rises
As we age
Body sore
Sight of grave

Drumrolls finish
Sluggish pace
Savior carries us
Last leg of the race

To our eternal home
Our true resting place

Strength

My strength is sapped, I feel the breeze
I lie flat, breathe

Eyelids so heavy, dusk beckoning
Rest calling me

Fill me again with cool water
Gentle hand

Champion of day, pump air in lungs
Let my voice sing

Exuberance, vigor, shouts Deliverer
Exhale thanksgiving

In sleep, protect me from the unseen
Tempters reasoning

Nourish my body, soul, may peace
abide, hold

Restful Breath, Spirit fill my core, my limbs
Remove dryness

All for my Savior's name, give strength
to proclaim

VI.
STILLNESS

He says, 'Be still, and know that I am God; I will be exalted among the nations, I will be exalted in the earth.'

Psalm 46:10

Jubilant Array

The sea resounds
The stars burst forth
The trees clap
The tempest roars
The flowers open
The fish soar

The grasses sway
The ground shakes
The rocks split
The rainbows display
The deserts bloom
The darkness fades

The waters ripple
The wings chase
The lilacs praise
The oxen bow
The orphans hold
The widows now

Adorned with joy
World restored
A baby boy
Shepherds flock
Kings will kneel
Legions of Angels

A prophesy revealed
The seas resound
The tempest roars

Grasshoppers

We are but grasshoppers
Nestled in the dirt

Bounding up and down
To see the earth
To us the world is but grass
Vision blurred

We are but a morning mist
Dispersed by light
Fleeting in the shadows
Of the cool night

Drops of dew rising high
Towards heaven's sky
We are but lilies of the field
Stretched in summer

Brilliant beauties revealed
Breezes flutter
Petals turn pastel
yield Faded color

Thank you, Lord, that we are,
but you are I AM.

Chicken Noodle

Praise you, Lord
For the simplest of meals
For savory broth
And chicken that heals.
For noodles shaped
Like snowflakes
For butter crackers
A ginger shake
Brought by neighbors
Sprite, ginger soda
Ginger tea, empathy
A pleasant aroma
Praise healing
Praise for taste buds
Praise for soothing bubbles
Praise for food before bed.
Chicken Noodle Soup
A gift in a can.

Refresh

Door cracked
Screens on
Breeze in
Heart calm
Birds sing
Tulips peek
Sun warms
Spirit speaks
Joy, sweet,
Joy awakening
Hearts full
Fears breaking
Moment caught
Soul refreshed
Clear waters
Timely rest

Enough

Enough, all that's required
Enough, when things expire.
Enough, an ample amount
Enough, on whom I count.
Enough, abundant supply
Enough, when my soul cries.
Enough, plenty of mercy
Enough, when I am thirsty.
Enough, a full measure
Enough, a true treasure.
Enough, more than I need
Enough, Christ within me.

Ordinary

Lord help me to be ordinary
To yearn for your glory
Not dwell on my story

Give me enough, needs met
A cup of water
Soup before bed

Prosperity, Father, is a dangerous ploy
It can harden the heart
And seek to destroy.

Items are elevated, futures planned.
No more consulting
The Great I Am.

Lord help me to be ordinary.
Delight in simplest things.
To let my heart sing.

To tend the garden and gather food
To help a friend.
Have clothes that mend.

To tell of your extraordinary grace
To worship you daily
And seek your face.

Come

Come weary
Come meek
Come laden
Come seek

Listen laborer
Listen child
Listen wayward
Listen mild

Rest soul
Rest feet
Rest bud
Rest tree

Recall heaven
Recall rain
Recall the Savior
Recall your gain

Go forth in joy
Go forth fed
Go forth nourished
Go forth, led

Future Glory

Lashed by storm
Afflicted one
Bedrock shifts
The sand moves quick
Sinking slow
Looking upward
Rescue planned
Lifted hand
Rebuild, renew
Foundation laid
Sapphire stones
Stacked turquoise
Jeweled gates
Ramparts of ruby
Resting walls
Future glory
Student of the Lord
Peace assured

Eyes to See

Afternoon light warm
Direct it pours

It settles on branches
Leaves dancing

Warming brick
Layered in paint

Glistening on
Block windows

Rainbow on
Pigeon petals

Glory encased hair
Juice added to pear

Birds sing of these things
Lord discipline my eyes
To receive radiance here

Father's Arms

Rest we in arms secure
Tested, tried, endure
Promise of life
Promise of love
Father directs above
He holds the earth
He holds out hand
We drag toes in sand
He carries my tired legs
On shoulders broad
He brings me home
I am never alone
He guards my heart
He guards the hall
My Father is my All in All

God's Will

For the wind to blow
   Seeds disperse
For the sun to rise
   Glad's verse

For breeze sweet
   Encompassing me
For rain caught
   Provision brought

God's will to build
   God's will to till
God's will to produce
   God's will be still

God's will to write
   God's will to sit
God's will to rest
   God's will we forget

Help me discern your will today for
My mind, my hands, my feet, I pray.

ABOUT SARAH

Sarah Suzanne Noble graduated with her Masters in Architecture from Ball State University in 2008. She practiced architecture and design, played 16" softball, led a Christian book club and tutored inner city kids before both writing and children entered her life.

This book is Sarah's second volume of poetry, the first being *I Cry Unto You, O Lord* (Cladach, 2019).

She currently lives, writes and creates in Chicago. Her artwork and writing go hand in hand. She is always creating and experimenting with new mediums. To follow her latest works on Instagram search for @sarahsuzannenoble.

For fourteen years Sarah and her husband, Jonny, have attended Park Community Church in Chicago. They are involved in several ministries including marriage mentoring and crisis support. They have two children, Ruthie age eight and Jacob age six.

Sarah comments: "Special thanks to Jonny for reading everything I write, to my friends who help me wonder, and to my parents for the firm foundation on which I stand."

I CRY
unto
YOU,
O LORD

poems of lament

SARAH SUZANNE NOBLE